A la carte

Poetry from a bipolar mind

Drew K Swindells

Grosvenor House
Publishing Limited

This book is published by
Grosvenor House Publishing Ltd
Link House
140 The Broadway, Tolworth, Surrey, KT6 7HT.
www.grosvenorhousepublishing.co.uk

A CIP record for this book
is available from the British Library

ISBN 978-1-80381-921-1
eBook ISBN 978-1-80381-922-8

About the Author

I live in Buckinghamshire, UK.

I've been writing poetry for around three years when my girlfriend at the time got me interested.

Since then, I've developed my voice and write mainly about mental health, love and lost love.

I love highly emotional pieces that pack a punch and somewhat old-fashioned romance!

I was diagnosed with bipolar affective disorder a long time ago and draw on my experiences and feelings.

I use a pen name sometimes, 'the Manic Poet'. I also introduce the semi-colon into my work. It's a mental health symbol meaning survival, i.e., an author could have used a full stop but decided to carry on instead.

'Gold and silver', a metaphor, also makes some appearances.

Drew K Swindells

Contents

Chapter 1 (Lunatic fringe)

Insane

Time in a bottle, my life in a verse,
reality overload, I feel I could burst.
I chant with the Angels before it gets worse.
My eyes are wide and staring, my knuckles are bruised.
I'm quite insane now, with nothing to lose.

Moods

I live a dichotomy, a two-dimensional life.
It takes some getting used to
I have settled in quite nice.
I have paisley on one wall, the other has nice stripes.
I have a plain girlfriend out of town and a sexy one that gripes.
I have two of most things in a practical sort of way;
I have a swinging mood disorder and I live it every day.

Treasure

My tarnished box of treasures
is exposed for all to see
a life so full of promise
but little dignity
People came to use me
and set me up to fail
but I had several dreams
that I would not let them steal
The Angels and the devils
came to play with my mind
but I always kept a part of me
buried so deep inside
My friends are now all crazy
yet they all understand
I have little more of value
and not much to leave behind.

'Poor mental health #1'

In the far north on the ice floes
chilled to the bitter bitter bones.
A white-out for a week a month
right now, I'm way out to lunch.
In the end in turmoil and confusion
the wolves came to feast on
all my nightmare and illusion.
At last, I was at peace;

Bag for life

God gave me a bag for life and filled it with my dreams.
He counted them in one by one and again one after the other.
Trusty, comforting, reliable, used for their warm familiarity,
Later worn out, unfulfilled, abused for their overfamiliarity.
It's hard to let them go, as is the cooling late summer,
full of the easy broken promises we told to one another.

Contrail of tears v2

A spider's web of such detail
can exist in a dying contrail
In a sky of monochrome madness,
a black and white web of kind and sadness.
Morning embers are stoked and caught, warms my day and
warms your heart.
Somewhere near a baby cries, somewhere near and someone
dies.
Madness is a comfort blanket
in the chaos of a drunken banquet.
Your love once washed over me and saved me from insanity;

Dreams and bedlam

Broken hearts and broken dreams
send me back to manic themes
Episodes and mothballed fears
misunderstood to float on tears

Seven things I won't forget
astronauts and a beloved pet
You and I in love that year
a magical place that's still in here

Sleepless nights and pointless strife
worry about my long-lost life
panic attacks that leave me crashed
Monday morning and always trashed

Dreams and nightmares v2

I'm living in a nightmare seeking succour in a dream
reality keeps waking me and poisoning my brain
So I cry for people I don't know and avoid some I do
is this the reality of lockdown for me for them for you?
I can manipulate reality right inside my head
be your perfect lover or a coffee morning friend
Play out that sweet scene and make it right this time
then I come out of it back to the daily grind
Carefree summer days that rolled on and on and on
jam sandwiches and bike rides life was always fun
The first time I kissed a girl, summer of '64
two innocents riding a wave as it crashed upon the shore
Not yet grown but no longer a child,
life was in a sweet spot, a wild mysterious time.

Dystopian worlds

If you look inside my head
you find a landscape so bereft
the awful waste of empty space
the emptiness of now

If you look inside my life
you find a landscape of tragic strife
opportunity sits on rubbish tips
the loneliness of now

If you look inside this world
you find a landscape of endless hurt
broken promises on sinners' crosses
the ruination of now

Suffer
Bob Dylan mashup (desolation row)

It's hurting bad, I don't know why
I want to but I cannot cry.

In the sunshine of your mind
in the moonbeams of my heart
a thought escapes the pain
and one more false start.
And nobody has to think too much about
(Desolation Row)

Remember when you suffer
and your head is full of hurt
someone somewhere loves you
and wants to wash away your dirt.
Don't send me no more letters, no
unless there from
(Desolation Row)

If you look inside this world
you find a landscape of endless hurt
broken promises sit on sinners' crosses
the ruination of now.
As Lady and I look out tonight from
(Desolation Row)

Bipolar Angels

The pressure of speech is now within reach
a cacophonic choir raising hell.
Empty a bottle to drown out my ears
raise a glass to my old, battered fears.
The manic Angels are out playing tonight
on wings of gold and silver delight.
Heads up to madness I've been here before
tossed on that brutal, beautiful shore.

Endless night

In another dark night of the soul
I face my demons on a roll
laugh or cry?
sob and pray?
for forgiveness?
a brand-new life?
or just another day?
who cares if I live or die?
in another dark night of the soul

Will Love take away my cold stinging tears?
to be a soft blanket for my hard jagged fears?
When colour returns to all that's dark black
the gold and silver doves of reason fly back

Hell at midnight (this time again) v2

Open up my hell at midnight,
decorate with my oldest fears
those familiar scenes of pain,
sweetest degradation again.
Drugs don't work this time,
I'm bouncing off the walls again
I'm hiding in the corners again
panic attacking my gut again.
I'm taking it (this time again).
I'm hiding it (this time again).
I'm crying (this time again).
I'm dying (this time again).
As the clock strikes twelve
with no one around
I'm hiding on the ceiling
till the sun brings me down.

can.i get.a.break.this.time?

At the palace

Down the rabbit hole with Alice
we have dreams of life at the palace.
I'm her King she's my Queen
the juggler forever entertains us.
The triggers that keep us going
by daytime keep on growing
the blocks that need more treatment
making the strongest statement.
Madness is a state of mind
not so easy to leave behind
in the beginning it's a woozy
far away from the daily grind.
Me and Alice at the palace
drinking Pepsi and snorting Coke
telling jokes to the royal folks
dragging on a massive toke.

Hope

In the back of beyond and
my hope is all gone and
I'm sucking on dirt just
to rid me of hurt.
Judge me your worst and
it will justify your first and
fucking my head sane
with a hammer again.
I strain on my pain again and
again.
Don't label me faulty (I always feel guilty) (enough);

Jab my heart

Scratch my nerves lockdown style,
fill my senses, make me smile,
tease my eyes, engage my wits,
kill my dreams, such a bitch.

In the past grind my ease,
Covid bugs make me sneeze,
jab my heart then jab my arm,
all is right but never calm
In the dark at 4 am
nightmares end and demons come,
play that tune that sweet refrain
I am wrong about so many things.

Alone at last behind a mask,
my heart rests awhile inside your smile.
along the shore of dream and more,
to meet behind love's long locked door;

Mediocrity

Born to the comforts of mediocrity,
dead to the eons to come.
Voluptuous clouds of indifference,
my life another messed up one.
If God or Satan come calling,
don't know if to rise up or fall?
Hard jagged clouds of oblivion,
or dead to the universes to come?

Memories v3

The heavy hand of obscurity
weighs upon my mind
people do not know me
or what I left behind.
The stresses and strains of living
have kicked me in the head
I took some pills and platitudes
and changed my mind instead.
Now living in a two-bed flat
big telly on the wall
the tv people talk to me
with memories of you.
Mental health is mental
it does my head right in
mood swings are not swinging
they trap me like some sin.
Conversations in my head
with a stranger a dog and a friend
all together for hours on end
it drives me round the bend.

Numbers in life and death

The six sides to sanity
and half a dozen new pearls
I die seven times in the night's emphatic verse.
Sometimes I win the game of love and sometimes I get cursed
sometimes it's a normal dream but sometimes it's much worse.
So, join me in my ramblings
it's a nice place to be
people can judge my simple acuity.
The six sides to sanity have come to smother me
The half a dozen pearls are lost on the shore
and my death has come for me as I walk again in awe.

Ode to bipolar #23

I've come to the end of the tracks and been read the riot acts.
I've had some bad times and I've had some sad times and I've
had some times full to brimming with bliss.
I've had some glad times and I've had some mad times, but the
best times were always with you.
I tried to be good, and I try to be better but, in the end, I've
had to settle (with you).

One of them places

My aunt is in one of them places,
where they try to find traces
of how she used to be back when.
She looks at me like she should know me,
puts on her smiley face for me,
flickers of remembering light up her eye.
We make conversation with her,
shed a hidden tear for her,
she's trying to make sense with a busted, broken tool.
Back then I'm drinking her tea,
listening to stories about my family,
her far-away days shrinking like morning mists.
I have my memories of her
Christmases and shopping trips with her
fixing her telly and other broken stuff.

but I can't fix her

I love it when my moods match the weather

Defeated, I let the rain in my heart run down my face. Uplifted, I imagine the summer sun massaging pleasure into my tired aching body.

Parrot

Got a parrot on my shoulder biting my ear,
reminding me about my past full of misery, lust and fear.
Got a black dog in my heart, eating my soul
like a load of cold porridge in a huge, massive bowl.
Does anyone even know? Does anyone care?
Will they come like I'm in an asylum?
come for a damn good stare?
Misery loves misery so they say, so I avoid everyone, I duck
dive and pray,
begging once again for a better, happy day.

Poor mental health #8

1;
Escalate my savoir faire, eliminate my neg
stop the small town ever stare, let me hide away
2;
Tv dinners, picking winners
the bachelor life, retired it's nice
on my own in my two-bed flat
near the shops, it's nice like that
eating four cornettoes on the trot
six sausage rolls, wow that's a lot!
my life is pleasant I can say
dying bit by bit, dying day by day

Cake

Bipolar is my nemesis
I can never shake
God was making crumpets
I came out like cake
the lows are crap the highs a bitch
the middle bits are boring
The docs have tried to do their thing
but they can never restore me

Extremes

A lonely road that has one end
arrow straight without a bend.
You and I a step apart
full of dread in head and heart.
Anxiety rules with stubborn will
setting concrete flows to fill
the spaces and creative crack
that gives my mind a little slack.
Eventually sleep comes to mend,
restores my sanity once again,
rituals played out in my life
in loops of extreme joy and strife.

Spiders

Spiders in corners and flashes of Angel wing
in the heartlands in the middle of retrospecting,
Double denim and triple black
puts me on edge and sends me back.
Back in the day when we were on track
carefree childhoods and friends who gave us slack.
Stress now has us tight and anxious
in this bubble of double talk so fractious.
Now I'm reaping what I sow and it sucks like rush,
sleep eludes me cos I think too much.

Suffering

Why do people suffer?
said the Chinaman to the fly
if I had created everything
I would have let it slide on by.
The fly created everything
but is also nothing much,
just another way to put
an itch in a dog's crotch.
I did create reality, said the dirty fly,
suffering was an afterthought
and I can't remember why.

Memories

Family holidays and memories,
San Francisco to Los Angeles:
I had a panic attack;
someone brought clam chowder back.

The asylum

In the asylum at midnight
I can't take it no more.
I bounce off the ceiling
and sleep on the floor.

Time has no meaning,
it's relatively stretched,
every nano an hour
ain't life a bitch?

Then last October
I'm stressed out and blue
in prison (solitary) lockdown,
was it the same for you?

Insanity squanders time with regret.
(Found you in summer,
dated all fall,
split up in winter,
oh, what a fool.)
Reality reboot and a harder reset?

As the clock strikes twelve
with no one around
I hide on the ceiling
till the sun brings me down;

can.i.get.a.break.this.time?

The boondocks #3

You put me in the boondocks
with your acid tongue and bile
you put me in the boondocks
you couldn't manage a smile
So now I'm in the boondocks
with my loving arms and guile
oh yes, I'm in the boondocks
without your wit and style
But I remember us in the boondocks
the cat and me and you
three more fruit loops in the boondocks
hurting like we do

The good things

The good things in my life go straight down the drain,
when black dog comes to visit again.
He gnaws at my mind with overwhelming despair,
he kicks me in the guts, that feels so unfair.
Swimming in blue with my head in a fug,
I've slipped into lethargy, a warm cloying fog.
So, I eat white pills, get ready for the better,
waiting for dark black to change into colour.

The green, green wood v2

In the green, green wood of endless dreams I have schemed so many schemes.
Some are schemes of better things, some half-remembered catastrophes.
Are your dreams the same as mine? twisted like a ball of twine
Spherical, tidy, yet a tangled mess,
twine waiting for use, for a test.
Abandoned in corners of lifeless souls,
unused like so many goals.
In the dark lonely wood of forgotten dreams.

The rabbit holes of anxiety

Down the rabbit hole with Mary
our triggers get quite hairy
mask my face it's out of place
my intentions are quite scary

My bias for panicked anxiety
now comes back to haunt me
the seven blocks that kill me
now wake me up to thrill me

The human condition we share
is hidden away from our stare
my soulmate will gaze in my heart
and erase what keeps us apart

A blues song

The blues is going to turn me
The blues is going to burn me
The blues is going to hurt me
inside out.
The blues is going to grind me
The blues is going to ride me
The blues is going to bind me
Right or wrong.

Watching telly

Up all night inside my head,
watching telly from my bed.
Viewing snaps of my life's randomness,
laugh or cry it's all the same mess.
My mind is skewed, I'm not like them,
It jumbles up now, the future and back then.
Unresolved illusions plague my life,
I chew on them, but they just give strife.
Folks who offer their worn-out platitude,
their brains are working as was meant to.
I can't listen it's all too much,
my life has no meaning it's out of touch.
No sleep, no relief and no respite,
is this what madness feels like?

A bipolar life

(Back then)
Young and discovering life's secret promise,
chasing pure threads of silver and gold.
Drawing me toward life's hidden meaning,
twinkling promises of just out of reach.
(Back then)
Mental illness was my life's roller coaster.
Finding gold and silver strands of life's hidden treasure.
Depths of despair, heights of manic pleasure,
forever insatiable and out of control.
(Back then)
Then off on another weekend adventure.
Twisting gold and silver lust out of nothing but bold.
Welcomed and enjoying pure manic pleasures,
with my secret new and exciting weekend friends.
(Now)
Sat in a dull office being inspected and medicated once more,
a box of tissues for my bitter dead fears.
Too late I have complete understanding,
my exquisite silver and gold life trashed on the floor.

(Now)
Calm, comforted and cured
we are all living the same perfect existence.
At last we are all on the same medication,
blinking back the same dried-up dead tears.

The bipolar spectrum

Bipolar has a spectrum,
it's inside your head.
It makes you want to do things
like chat and fuck and spend.
Up all night like a line for free
it grinds you down and it grinds me.
Burning candles at both ends
live free, drop out, burnt out?

No hope for us and none for me.

Bipolar man
Elton John mashup (Rocket Man)

The rhythm of life, bastardised
I'm right up there, staring eyes.
I see it all, beyond the stars
in my heart my God dies.

Between the high places and the lows
is where my sanity hides, God only knows.
Pretend life is normal, pretend it flows
as I conjure up a thousand woes.

I'm not the man they think I am at home
Oh, no, no, no
burning out my fuse here all alone
I'm bipolar man.

Social Phobia

I have bipolar affective disorder
I have social phobia too
I've been self-isolating since 2002

Suburban excess v2

Exotic ladies, spaced out crazies
the passionate wannabes
are strutting the boulevards
of fabulous excess

The hotel kitchens are cooking
as the receptionists are booking
the blissed-out swingers
of suburban excess

The hot spots and flesh pots,
the one more fab dive
cool babes and matadors
getting caught in the vibe

The gigolos of pleasure
at the end of their tether
their smiles of satisfaction
a melancholic distraction

My manic-depressive obsessions
overwhelming yet shallow
my hyper-sexual fate
(intellectual it ain't)
empty my pockets with a big old heartache

Killing the blues

There's a death in the family,
It put a death in my heart
I can't stare it down
I can't see no more

I went blind in both eyes
I gone deaf in one ear
I got the blues for my birthday
Blues gonna roll around next year

I drink a little whisky
I drink a little beer
I'm just killing the blues
I'm just killing the blues

I'm killing the blues.
I'm killing the blues
I'm just killing the blues
Blues gonna roll around next year

Trigger warnings #4 v3

(Fade in)

My thoughts are tumbling
I can't shut them out,
I write down some words
I whisper and shout.

The way you laugh
like sunshine through broken glass
and that sparkle in your eye
somehow makes me forget I was ever shy.

We didn't need much
we were eternally blessed,
we forgot our ravaged pasts and
chose happiness instead.

Now I'm alone and you've gone
all that's left is this song
of bittersweet memories and lust
turned into haunting melodies of us.

The seven words of Love
in a world full of hate,
commit them to memory
before it's too late.

The tears of compassion
the dead eye of remorse
I wait in the moonlight
for them to take their course.

The world is a strange place,
It's on TV news,
you think you understand it
then it gives you the blues.

Tears are running to my lips
that salty taste again,
memories come flooding back
the pain is like a flame.

Remorse is a sad thing
memories of regret
my tears are dripping
and I cannot forget.

A factory reject in a bin full of scrap
I'm told God will forgive me and take it all back.

So let's have a killing spree we'll be
on the news bulletins
let's say it's about religion or the colour of our skins.

(Fade out)

Jumbled thoughts (of Ukraine)

The seven verses and the three curses,
conspiracy theories and a fake genius,
stories and analogues, pastiches and unicorns,
oblique references to a sensual paramour,
a babies smile and a lifetimes regret,
Kings and Queens and a short odds bet,
a missed appointment for medicinal ointment,
memories jumble as kingdoms tumble,
my pills and platitudes in a world full of failure,
a global catastrophe on my 200 quid telly,
a long-term panic attack that
just/keeps/fighting/back.

Bunker #2

In my bunker of secret desires
I set my locked up brutal fires,
burning for an eternity to the core,
in my mind's eye more, more, more.
Stoked by passion fuelled by hate
hidden away, out of the gate,
feed my flame feed my fire,
in my bunker of secret desire

Chapter 2 (Old school poet)

Angels # 24

Angels dancing two by two
on golden flakes of silver dew
simple music, composed above
a sacred tune for me, for love

Again, before v2

I dreamt of you
again, before
in deep gloss just the same
We knew each other
again, before
in pure green, lasting till dawn
We swam on the edge of time at the centre
again, before

And we laughed as our dreams came true;

The taste of love v2

I remember the taste of our love
ice cream and candy stolen from above.
I remember the taste of your skin,
honey and caramel, mixed up with sin.
I remember the taste of our fun
vanilla milkshake spilt in the sun.
Memories like hunger sated time and again
the past and the present ignited in flame.

Segued blues

As summer segued into fall
I lost my love, I lost it all
In a few short months or years,
dry my cheek then dry my tears
then I can walk tall
as another summer segues into fall

Lonely heart

A warm muggy day, middle of June
a rainy rainy Sunday afternoon
She opened her heart far too soon
she was never ready, it had been an age
So she put it back, turned the page
her lonely lonely heart trapped in its gilded cage

Blue days lonely nights

I go to the shops to see a face
missing you today in this cold sad place
I never realised you'd be missed this much
your smile, laugh and your touch
you've gone yet you're still here and there
I can't cry you back to feel my care
It hurts so much to feel so dead
in my heart and in my head
I feel the blues down in my soul
loneliness mocks my every goal

Mannequin

Resurrect my mannequin
make her bloom again
in the tangled brushwood
in the wilds where we had stood
Worship for my mannequin
let her bloom then bloom again
in her boudoir, she cried for love
for her faith and for her life
A tragedy and distorted views
TV bulletins, TV news
the breakups and the makeups
A broken heart that's just the start
forgiveness and a disjointed story
for the love, for the glory
Water cascades over me
emotions cascading, none can see
time cascades over me
a life cascading, for all to see.

In the suburbs of love

Sunday morning washing cars
mow the lawn then hit the bars
'In the suburbs of love',
play the parts we practised then
pushing dolly way back when
cowboys and Indians bam~bam~bam.
Future roles we learned so well
'In the suburbs of love'
and our provincial hell.

Mystery

Dripping diamonds like a queen
breaking hearts she's never seen
in and out of loves embrace
putting on her party face
in her mind as black as coal
she must build her one true wall
her intentions are a mystery
her vision only she can see
the sting of misery comes too soon
when she takes her fill of you

Oblivion

At the end of the world
at the gates of oblivion
I met you again, divine obsidian.
In pools of deep gloss
and lakes of pure green
we swim at the end of time
singing songs of redemption, divine.

Parody, Crash, Happiness, Utopia

Parody
A parody of passion
you copy what you've seen
she's frozen like a statue
and contemplates her tea

Crash
Blues tunes that kill the mood
you can leave them all behind you
but the car crash of your life
is right there still inside you

Happiness
Happiness walks beside you
it tidies up your mess
It makes you feel like a God
and leads to heavenly bliss

Utopia
Utopia and a craving
a feeling of our faith
we all hold onto perfection
although it's come too late

Past and future

We pose and prance and pirouette
down the years we can't forget
From a night as black as tar
to a dawn dreamt of from afar
Tears of joy that stain our faces
leave forever some bitter traces
Loneliness my true companion
down the years of desperation
Another new another start
this time we shall never part

Random #2

My brain is banging in my head
I'll never be the same
my heart has broken two by two
alcohol is not my friend

One amulet of friendship
lost in the mists of time
stolen by a jealous God
you're still a friend of mine

The love I lost in winter
replaced the fourth of June
we went to the movies
and held hands all through

I'm a reasonable man
my life is give and take
I want to seduce you
and skinny dip in the lake

A disapproving alcoholic
thinking oh, what the fuck
he can see right through me
my life will often suck

Summer spell

Lazy days in the fields,
my mind is open, my lips are sealed.
We ate our picnic, talked and drank,
on the grass, just near the bank.
Our words danced on summer cloud,
plenty was said, not all out loud.
The storm came unexpectedly, broke the spell,
we promised we would never tell.

Us

I left the big city
moved to the sticks
now I am without you
I am breaking hearts like twigs

We were an item
yea, a two for one
we knew what really mattered
and the sex was lots of fun

We couldn't have kids
we blamed each other
now you've moved out too
and live with your sweet lover

Wings

Flying through the night on wings made of bold
I embrace you on the other side of midnight once more.
We laugh as we live out our secret love lives
forgotten as the dust is rubbed from our eyes.

We have seen the moon

I can open up my heart
and I can spill my guts
I can break your heart in two
because you care so much

You're such an easy target
You're oh so open too
we are like one another
we have seen the moon

A vision in the moonlight
compassion from a seer
laughter on a carrier wave
I have felt them near

Passion in a heartbeat
a wolf cries at the moon
the human condition is lonely
and we all die far too soon

Blue eyes

The bluest sea of salty tears
enchanting like my lover's eyes.
Eyes that held a thousand fears
a thousand more exquisite sighs.
A jealous God denied for years
exacts revenge in brutal guise.
The Covid ward then disappears

The final act to.close.her.eyes.

Blood

1st;
The cards you sent to me
are now in the back of a drawer;
they break my heart so much
I can't read them anymore.
2nd;
In the winter when the sun goes down
I'm still pounding this dirty old town,
no one looks and no one cares
then I'm down and everyone stares.
It's all so sad it's as sad as fuck
I'm down on my heels and out of luck.
3rd;
The twelve apostles and the virgin Mary
welcome another sinner wide eyed and scary.
Redemption is the battle cry, over and over
but they never say why.
4th;
Back in the day when everything mattered,
back in the day when blood was splattered,
life had meaning and I walked tall,
I marched in the streets for the good of all.
5th;
Now I'm dying and all alone
here and now my memories flicker
here and now and I hear the sniggers.

The Manic Poet

Entanglement v2

Hearts and minds can entwine
in the second hand of time.
Finding love among the dust
of broken lives and mistrust.
All that passion all that lust
wasted on my wheel of rust.
True romance and a lover's vow
have more meaning right here right now.

Feelings

I wish my feelings were dispensable
I'd scoop my heart out like a receptacle
I thought you loved me for eternity
but it only lasted to 6:30 (pm);

C'est la vie

Why?

She drips her love into my ear
as I quaff my second beer
I stroke her fragile ego too
her pain it helps to soothe
The wrinkles on her heart I smooth
and help her with a brand-new start

Because we are in love

The horizon

The pastel colours of old love
lie quiet on the horizon.
Our love lies there for all to see.
Beyond is a new horizon where
you and I will forever be
entwined in a pastel dream.

Kisses, wishes, misses

Eleven kisses, a dozen wishes
twenty-three longed for near misses
I walk the barren earth to find
that which once was left behind
I count out loud the eleven kisses
count again the dozen wishes
hoping to find the one who knows me
the only one who can complete me

Lockdown blues #44

Sex and sandwiches and cups of tea
are the things I remember most about
(You and me)
Back in the day before the fall
(You and me)
were the life and the soul
Now you're gone and the world's off key
we're in lockdown, no more
(You and me)

My first

Time in a bottle, my life in a verse
I go to the beginning to capture my first.
My first kiss,
my first heartbreak
my first universe of hope.
When you capture a butterfly,
when you capture a bird,
to say they don't matter is plainly absurd.

I remember you

I remember you
back then.
Back in our day with inky fingers
and big plans and no idea
back then.
Schoolyards and pigtails
shy smiles and mysteries
back then.
In our past another country
I remember my first love
back then
and I remember you.

Lost love

Weep my tears, sigh my sighs
show the world how very wise
She has gone, into that bottle
her memory gone but not forgotten,
delete her photo, erase her passion
replace her love with an imitation

One day she will sit easy in my past
till then a 4 am shadow she will cast

Love symbols

The precious gold and silver symbols of their love were hidden in the heavens for all to see.
Look carefully and you may glimpse them in midwinter when the moon casts her long shadows.

Memories

I saw your smile in a broken mirror
heard your song on the wind.
I called your number: 'disconnected'
guess you don't want to be found.
I see broken hearts all around me.
Everything's sad now you've gone.
Guess I will try to forget you;
guess I will dream of you again.

Modern love

In the automatic laundromat
where people come to hide,
I fell in love when you caught my eye.
Smooth textured like a Goddess, sensually appealing.
I sighed inside and fell in love with love's truest meaning,
Life is for living, love is for giving,
take it, break it, but never ever fake it.

Monday weeks

Monday weeks, nothing speaks
Alone at last behind a mask
my heart rests awhile inside your smile
our love forged divine once more in rhyme
Along the shore of dream and more
to meet behind love's long locked door

Our Arcadia

Welcome to Arcadia,
our paradise found,
living in the moment
the beauty of new now.
Actualising dreams
reality unbound,
flying over moonbeams
tripping on pure sound.

More moods #29

A lonely road that has one end
arrow straight without a bend
you and I a step apart
full of dread in head and heart

Anxiety rules with stubborn will
setting concrete flows to fill
the spaces and creative crack
that gives my mind a little slack

Eventually sleep comes to mend
restores my sanity once again
Rituals are played out in my life
in loops of extreme joy and strife

Death knells

My love is in the death knells
I'm online treading on eggshells
my body is crying so bad
I'm feeling much worse than just sad

Rhinestones

The broken rhinestones of my life are scattered in the dirt
The broken memories of you back then will bring back all
my hurt
We broke the rules, the seven sins
flew too high and burnt our wings
to the end of our exquisite starts

Now worn out, broken and blue

Rhythms v2

Dance in the arms of a stranger
passion is driving your sate
stolen love past midnight
rhythms are sealing your fate

Me and you on the dance floor
the zephyrs are acting real proud
the couples silent romancing
wish we could lose this crowd

Senses so sensually merging
love has come for you late
timeless patterns are stirring
rhythms are sealing your fate

Feelings on numb

Woke up too early, sick as a dog,
head in a spin rapid brain fog.
My mind is broken, body is too,
I remember too clearly when I fell out of love with you.
Cold sweats, callous bets.
Reach for a bottle, drown out regrets.
Hard drinking continues, feelings on numb.
Here I am again, what's to become?

I whisper for forgiveness, I cannot shout.

Two hearts

Trace my heart in paper fine
put with yours & stamp 'divine'.
Love, the glue that sticks together,
in a dream that lasts forever.

The shore

Life and death are simple twists
dappled lights on water glints.

On the shore of emerald green
we talk alone of what has been.

Memories are made of this
washed out emotions, candy sticks.

People walking on the shore
conversations heard, not recalled.

A reality of perfection in my head
when all is done, and all is said.

You and I walking, talking more
on that elusive emerald shore.

Take me

take me to the edge and show me the blue river
take me to the edge and let me see the gold and silver
take me to the edge and let me look down
take me to the edge of time
so I won't be alone

Wishing

wishing my wishes were real to you
wishing I was with you, not blue not blue
wishing I could find a way to melt your heart
wishing your wishes didn't break mine apart
after this madness, wishes can come true

Wishing

wishing wishes
wishing wishes can
wishing wishes can come
wishing wishes can come true
heaven in a kiss every memory of this

and we will find more bliss than ever dreamt of

Tuesday's moon of love

Two hearts speaking truth to last,
love laid bare, a vision
under Tuesday's moon of love.

Hearts beat faster as dreams are shared
the past is banished, love looms large
under Tuesday's moon of love.

Wings of love

In times gone past
grand dreams could last
but now they crash and die

Imaginings could fly on wings
now they stagnate with age
to die upon the forgotten page

Alone again with tear stained eyes
heavy heart and heavy sighs
contemplating what might have been.

A blood-stained dove on wings of love
her destiny fulfilled in heaven above.
on broken hope she'll fly too high

the Angel of mercy rewards her.

Chapter 3 (Life and death etc.)

Market life

The sparrow in the market
eating for two,
she's got her healthy eating plan
though she's poor all through.
Apples and plums
some green to score,
her boy is a skinny chugger, two to four.
He's from down old Camberwell way,
the dogs and the birds eat up all his pay.
Hiding away, attracting stares
the love they share is going nowhere.

My skinny girl in the market,
scoring some fruit and gear.
I'll be there on Monday,
chugging for easy money then disappear.
Thursday at the dogs the birds all love me cos I'm on a
winning streak.
By Sunday it's all long pockets and fake,
Emptied out by one more losing streak.

Dead soldiers v2

The body bags are coming back
to the homeland black on black.
Drums beat for the brave
the widows and the ashes
Spiralling numbers on endless news flashes.

Ten years later a tourist trap
plastic flags and suchlike crap,
Burnt out tanks, selfie backdrops,
dusty feet in dirt cheap flip flops.

Supermarket

In the supermarket of Covid panic
the online slots are always tragic
They pile up their baskets of greed
to check out their 2-for-1 need
Panic buys and overspending
in the land of never ending
Get on board this train of lust
stand in line without a fuss

Genesis

All my tomorrows crashed today
revealing all my yesterdays,
all the way back to genesis.

I saw you back there past the veil,
destinies entangled but quite pale,
as time fractured reality cracked.
You were here and had my back.

Random #1

A day trip to the dales
passengers on a bus
a girl that once broke my heart
there wasn't a lot of fuss

The eagle-eyed inspector
craning for a view
the three local magistrates
sitting in judgement of you

A queue in the ocean fish bar
a Friday night in June
the Italian ice cream seller
my childhood over too soon

Madness dwells within me
it snuck up way back when
it stuck a finger in my head
and said 'so sorry my friend'

The golden strands of beauty
the silver strands of love
twist them to an effigy
and worship from above

There was a choir of Angels
they sang in my ear
I was transfixed for seven hours
and cried without a tear

The alley

The alley between life and death
is a place between dreams and despair
it's an unpretentious simple place
where I go to follow and stare

All my yesterdays and tomorrows
are set out with compassion and care
for the alley between life and death
is a place full of vision and flare

The Angels and devils will plague me
in the alley between life and death
my mind I used to rely on
deserts me between dream and despair

The wise men and the shepherd
shall knock upon my door
and ask if I am ready to face
the last thing that I can endure

The poetry and the prose

Poetry for pleasure
puts you in a spell
open up your heaven
before it turns to hell

The vicar in his vestry
vespers start at three
he genuflects and whispers
and sees through you and me

The lightning struck twice
the day that we both left
the thunder cracked on and on
as it rolled in from the west

The mortuary attendant
has seen it all before
he fills out all the paperwork
then cleans blood off the floor

The amulets of friendship
scattered in the past
the tears of life's losses
failures that will last

A life to forget

Take a walk down lonely street
to the boulevard of broken dreams
you'll find suicide alley there
unremarkable as it seems

Ten cents in one pocket
a coat from the mission
a belly full of charity
was this your life vision?

She took you for every cent
and laughed in your face
all your friends deserted you
the day you fell from grace

Now at the end of your tether
as you stare at a rope
nowhere else to turn my son
and no more blessed hope

They will find you in the morning
stand around no doubt and stare
and wonder why you did it
at last, someone will care

Death in the family

Platitudes and preaching
I'm worn out with dead speeching.
No way I'm willing as my red eyes keep filling.
So sorry for your loss, sir,
step into the car, sir,
whisked off to the pub, sir,
for alcohol and chat, sir.
Later it's me and the cold dead telly,
monochrome memories to last lifetimes,
tears to fill an ocean.

Covid aftermath

The skinny inbetweeners
The chronic irredeemers
The sinnin' artful dodgers
The ones who can quote sonnets
Don't mean a thing when the tears start flowin'.

The widows of the pacemakers
who could see it all coming.
The aftermath of a tragedy
Now everyone is running from
The floods are flowing free
And it's unavoidable and so real.

Grief

A few of us, not much is said
my tears are falling on her bed
to claw back time, I try and fail,
I pray so hard but she's still pale
time has stopped to start my grief
my heart is empty and no relief

Numbers in my window

Two red kites flying free,
owning the sky majestically.
Two squirrels in fighting mood,
squabbling for each other's food.
Two crows like soldiers at attention,
proud in a square-bashing session.
Two magpies in formal gear,
black tie at the opera with no fear.
Waiting for snow one lone robin,
in Christmas card pose

with two cold legs throbbing.

Perfection

Terraform a planet make it just like here,
create a perfect paradise where we all live without fear.
In this pretty paradise we can all rule like gods,
the people will be just like us with happy healthy bods.
Lots of pretty animals perform at our feet,
don't worry how they get turned into meat.
We go to the country for our mental health,
no one cares about not having any real wealth.
If we turn our planet of perfection into an eye-sore,
don't stress about it my friend we can just terraform an (awful)
lot more.

21st century blues

Detox your life before it's too late
your mind and body will con.tam.in.ate
with this 21st-century world of hate,
in this land of once regal forces
now shaken with impossible choices
people screaming with masked voices.
A new kind of life we could all choose
untainted with these 21st century blues
gold and silver tomorrows we will never lose

(online) Haters v2 (Euro 2020)

The mirror cracked
no going back
The mood of hatred
darkness, sated
The innocent and the gifted
wasted by the haters, listed
In the spirals of despair
ashamed to see, ashamed to stare

Rhymer's block

Triple black and double denim
dead inside is just the beginning.
Never mind the spider's curse
never mind the third and fourth verse.
The rhymers block that stops you resting
the seven seas that keep you guessing.
The April Fools and the great pretenders
the drunken banquet and a lovers' tryst.
All are here to entertain you,
in the aftermath of the greatest myth.

Shore of dreams and despair

On another warm moonlit night
I set sail on that sea of gold and silver delight.
God gave me a guide and a compass set fair
and an empty bag that was named 'despair'.
The compass broke upon the floor
my battles raged through rough and poor,
the bag named despair could hold no more
and my will broke on that brutal beautiful
shore.

Snapshots in my weekend (Saturday)

Sat in a cafe with a steaming cuppa,
eavesdropping on snaps of people's lives another and another.
Remembering the good times when I laughed and cooked soup for you
always with a taste of love, a taste of love for you.
Alone in that busy cafe swallowing down my fears,
I turn away once more to hide my secret tears.

Two universes/cop2026

Memories and mayhem and time to choose
pollution and scrap, yesterday's news
last week's universe with plenty to lose
dull and tarnished by too much hard news.
New beginnings in a universe of tomorrow
beautiful concepts without sadness or sorrow
spreading wings on the winds of the morrow
fly like my love to a place we can follow

Simple pleasures

I used to puff on cigarettes
behind the sheds in schoolyard bets.
Now a thousand empty packs
a thousand more turned to plaque.
My lungs are black, I am blue,
packs of pleasure saw me through.
Now broken body, broken heart,
simple pleasures, till death do us part.

War

Twenty-four lead soldiers line up in a row.
They fall over one by one,
such a tragic blow.

The armistice comes too late for all the millions dead.
The widows in their weeds cry for what was said.

The mustard gas looks pretty as it rolls around the fields.
The terrified soldiers are swallowing down their fears.

The poppy seller down the shops has his break for tea.
He never talks about his brother and everything they've seen.

What others have said about my poetry

'Incredibly evocative and powerful.'

'A magnificent write, Drew!'

'This is profound! I love every line!'

'Brilliant.'

'A gorgeous and brilliant write.'

'Your awesome inks bleed from your soul and the heart you wear on your sleeve.'

www.ingramcontent.com/pod-product-compliance
Lightning Source LLC
Chambersburg PA
CBHW032008040426
42448CB00006B/535